Once Upon A Dream

An Enchanted Symphony

Edited By Lynsey Evans

First published in Great Britain in 2024 by:

YoungWriters
Est. 1991

Young Writers
Remus House
Coltsfoot Drive
Peterborough
PE2 9BF
Telephone: 01733 890066
Website: www.youngwriters.co.uk

All Rights Reserved
Book Design by Ashley Janson
© Copyright Contributors 2024
Softback ISBN 978-1-83565-388-3

Printed and bound in the UK by BookPrintingUK
Website: www.bookprintinguk.com
YB0588R

FOREWORD

Welcome Reader, to a world of dreams.

For Young Writers' latest competition, we asked our writers to dig deep into their imagination and create a poem that paints a picture of what they dream of, whether it's a make-believe world full of wonder or their aspirations for the future.

The result is this collection of fantastic poetic verse that covers a whole host of different topics. Let your mind fly away with the fairies to explore the sweet joy of candy lands, join in with a game of fantasy football, or you may even catch a glimpse of a unicorn or another mythical creature. Beware though, because even dreamland has dark corners, so you may turn a page and walk into a nightmare!

Whereas the majority of our writers chose to stick to a free verse style, others gave themselves the challenge of other techniques such as acrostics and rhyming couplets.

Each piece in this collection shows the writers' dedication and imagination – we truly believe that seeing their work in print gives them a well-deserved boost of pride, and inspires them to keep writing, so we hope to see more of their work in the future!

CONTENTS

Canning Street Primary School, Newcastle Upon Tyne

Isha Rahman (10)	1
Hannah Cant (10)	2
Rayan Ahmed (10)	3
Lavinia Gurlea (10)	4
Denisa Singh (9)	5

Canon Barnett Primary School, London

Saaher Ahmed (6)	6
Zaheen Chowdhury (7)	7
Yusuf Sadek (6)	8

Cobham Free School, Cobham

Florence Mann (8)	9
Audrey Stephens (9)	10
Maya Haluszczak (8)	12
Umarah Choudhury (8)	13
Arthur Banks (8)	14
Amelia Murrle Milhac (9)	15
Evangeline Scanlan (8)	16
Oscar Hodgetts (8)	17
Elsie Carter (9)	18
Alexa Rayment (9)	19
Oscar França (8)	20
Genie Fraser (8)	21
Amaris Crova (9)	22
Michelle Botnarenco (9)	23
Breandan-James O'Connell (9)	24
Harriet Druce (8)	25
Elizabeth Cooper (8)	26
Darcey Dwyer (8)	27

Marlie Scianna (8)	28
Grace Mickleburgh (8)	29
Michael Lancaster (8)	30
Haris Ali Khan (8)	31
Eme Buckle (9)	32
Molly McBride (8)	33
Vincent Bashford (8)	34
Hamish McAllister (8)	35
Amber Rayment (9)	36
Jake Palmer (8)	37
George Stevens (8)	38
Farah Mallindine (8)	39
Mimi Barker-Dickson (8)	40
Elise Field-Rocks (8)	41
Gracie Parfitt (9)	42
Bella Barker-Dickson (8)	43
Jude Monaco-Houghton (9)	44
Illy Alushi (8)	45
Jess Harman (8)	46
Abigail Walker (9)	47
Harry McKenna (9)	48
Amelia Butler (9)	49
Logan Simpson (8)	50
Rafferty Liguorish (9)	51

Gawber Primary School, Barnsley

Olivia Parry (10)	52
Emily Brotherton (10)	53
Max Hill (10)	54
Jaiden-mai Skelley (10)	56
Jacob Thistlewood (9)	57
Erin Maunsell (9)	58
Charlotte Brayford (9)	59
Ava Woodhead (10)	60
Seb Crossfield (9)	61

Jenson Wilde (9)	62
Henry Hays (10)	63
George Bentley (9)	64

Heath Park School, Wolverhampton

Sonam Bansal (11)	65
Chantelle Sliwa (11)	66
Jana Abdullah (12)	67
Ara Amedi (12)	68
Henry Neale (12)	69

Ironville And Codnor Park Primary School, Nottingham

Parker Christensen (9)	70
Elijah Coope (11)	72
Rhys Finney (10)	73
Freddie Hendy (9)	74
Alexis-Leigh Hale (11)	75
Bobby Squares (9)	76
Ava-Grace Proctor (11)	78
Lacie-Anne Robinson (11)	79
Kaeden Akers (10)	80
Darcie Squires (10)	81

New Road Primary School, Sowerby Bridge

Ruby Watts (10)	82
Evie Potts (10)	83
Arabella Haleywood (11)	84
Daisy Brocklehurst (10)	85
Eliza Siwerska (10)	86
Poppy Prescott (11)	87
Iris Parkinson (11)	88
Finn Stephenson (10)	89
Lainy Bolton (11)	90
Maisie Smith (10)	91
Lexi Churchward (10)	92
Jack Jackson (11)	93
Lexie Quigley (11)	94
Mason Collier (11)	95

Zac Woodyatt (10)	96
Lincoln Taylor (10)	97
Eva Taylor (11)	98

Newington Community Primary School, Ramsgate

Henry Pepper (10)	99
Jamie Ferguson (10)	100
Mollie Simpson (10)	103
Ocean Perry (11)	104
Henry Harmes (10)	106
April Bradshaw (10)	107
Bella Bull	108
Freya Holt (10)	109
Millie Lambert-Robins (11)	110
Taylia Baker (11)	111
Charlie Cox (11)	112
Sofia-Dolce Adams (11)	113
Kirsten Valentina Tschirschky-Okoro (11)	114
Alfy Allen (11)	115
Max Teyn (11)	116
Aziell Ong (11)	117
Theo Usman (11)	118
Holly-Anne Vine (10)	119
Abigail Smith (10)	120
Max Booker (10)	121
Scarlett (11)	122
Daisy Lilley (11)	123
Olivia Cameron (10)	124
Poppy Lowe (10)	125
Lillie Gould (11)	126
James Smith (10)	127
Mason Chadd (10)	128
Michael Safronov (11)	129

Rackheath Primary School, Rackheath

Honey Allard (9)	130
Harrison Petts (10)	131
Connor Appleton (9)	132
Rachel Bryan (10)	133

Isaac Rynn (10)	134
Emily Thoulass (10)	135
Maxwell Sweatman (9)	136

Sarum St Paul's CE (VA) Primary, Salisbury

Imogen Eyres (10)	137
Grace Bugden (9)	138
Grace Parsons (10)	140
Evie Monington (10)	141

Springwood Federation (Junior School), Waterlooville

Darcey Doran (10)	142
Kinley Speake (10)	143
Eli Humphris (10)	144
Arabella Capell (10)	146
Marley Roberts (10)	147
Medeea Sacuiu (9)	148
Lola Hill (10)	149
Niamh Hussey (10)	150
Delilah Dales (10)	151
Isaac Dixon (9)	152
Ano Musa (9)	153
Charlotte Parker (9)	154
Oscar Faux (9)	155
Macie Doughty (10)	156
Logan McKenzie (9)	157
Alfie Walker (10)	158
Dalton Gray (9)	159
Jack Humphreys (9)	160
Isabelle Merrett (10)	161
Kyler Speake (9)	162
Elsie Lewis (10)	163
Magda Formela (10)	164
Darius Kidykas (9)	165
Isaac Bennett (9)	166
Katherine Scott (10)	167
Max Northall (9)	168
Annie-May Lines (9)	169
Amelia Coombes (9)	170
Elise Goolty (10)	171

Ana Makepeace (10)	172
Scarlett Prince (10)	173
George Needham (9)	174
Frederick Carter-Brazier (10)	175
Louis Cole (10)	176
Phoebe Spencer (9)	177
Harry Clements (10)	178
Madeleine Parker (9)	179
Mia Worcester (10)	180
George Johnson (9)	181

The Russell School, Rickmansworth

Florence Parker (10)	182
Theodore Peter Smith (10)	183
Ben Collett (10)	184
Emily Raine (10)	185

Widewell Primary School, Widewell

Lyla Keeling (10)	186
Jessica Cook (11)	188
Poppy Rebhan (11)	189
Chloe Ball (10)	190

Woburn Lower School, Woburn

Thea Gentry (9)	191
Harper Quinn Grady (7)	192
Malaki Godsall (9)	193
Hamish (9)	194
Freya Williams (9)	195
Olivia Smith (8)	196
Jake Farmer (7)	197
Logan Christie (8)	198
Genevieve Butler (9)	199
Katalea Butler (7)	200
Violet Whitmore (8)	201
Harley Walton-Payne (7)	202
Felix Howard (7)	203
Elodie Clarke (9)	204
Amy Bezh (7)	205

THE POEMS

What Is The Point Of War?

I came across a land.
But all I could see was rubble and sand.
My heart sank as I saw people evacuate from their own land.

Children are starving to death.
And still that continues to spread.
People are begging for something to eat.
And they have to witness their loved ones deceased.

Why do wars even exist?
All it causes is harm and other bad things.
I want to live in a world full of peace and happiness.
But this is what I get in return.

Isha Rahman (10)
Canning Street Primary School, Newcastle Upon Tyne

A Poem About My Mum

My mum is the best
She never has a rest and does her very best
She looks after me and my two sisters
And works hard each day getting me and my sisters up and dressed for school
Feeds my baby sister when she can't rest
Walks me and my sister to school in all different weather
She makes me food day and night
She makes me and my sisters happy
She is like a dream to me
And one day I will be able to be like her
And thank her for never giving up!

Hannah Cant (10)
Canning Street Primary School, Newcastle Upon Tyne

Race Strike

3, 2, 1... Pedal to the metal, accelerate with speed.
Make those wheels spin faster, then fly.
Let the wind guide you to the finish line,
As you drift on those turns and accelerate on the road.
Your fans are cheering to boost your confidence.
Accelerate with speed,
Win the championship for me and you.

Rayan Ahmed (10)
Canning Street Primary School, Newcastle Upon Tyne

I Am A Child

I am a beautiful child, smart and brave,
All day I play, I don't get bored at all.
I build and invent the stories I imagine,
And riddles I like and walks to the park.

I am always down to help
And at activities I have luck.
My mum and dad love me.
Next to them, I grow beautifully!

Lavinia Gurlea (10)
Canning Street Primary School, Newcastle Upon Tyne

School

I wake up and go to school,
It can be a useful tool.
As I go and show my moves,
You may go and show your grooves.
If you really missed your brain,
Please don't make it pour with rain,
If you're really in trouble,
Please don't do a massive grapple,
This is the end of school,
Hope you really find it cool.

Denisa Singh (9)
Canning Street Primary School, Newcastle Upon Tyne

Bear-Ly Escaping: A Tale Of Forest Adventure!

Once upon a time in a forest so deep,
where the trees stood so tall,
I stumbled upon a bear big and tall,
its fur was mighty, its eyes gleamed bright,
but I knew I had to escape with all my might.

With caution, I moved with care,
through the forest, unaware,
the trees whispered, the wind did blow,
as I tiptoed quietly, oh so slow.

I burst through the trees into the light,
having the bear out of sight,
I took a deep breath, feeling so alive,
grateful I managed to survive!

Saaher Ahmed (6)
Canon Barnett Primary School, London

Day At The Zoo

Last night I had a dream,
I went to the zoo and I had ice cream,
My daddy took us in his car,
Because it was very far.

We saw lots of animals at the zoo,
Lions, giraffes and zebras too,
The hippo was swimming,
And the cheetah was under the tree sleeping.

Seeing the chimpanzees was good fun,
As we walked under the burning hot sun,
I was feeling very happy
But my little brothers were sleepy.

At night my daddy drove us home in the car
And I looked in the sky to find a twinkling star.

Zaheen Chowdhury (7)
Canon Barnett Primary School, London

Ronaldo Scores

On the field out wide
Where football dreams and joy collide,
Cristiano Ronaldo, a shiny light scores a goal,
Siu takes flight, cheers erupt,
A sound echoes, dancing with the ball,
So neat, goals galore,
Oh what a feat!
With a kick so bright,
A rainbow hue,
Playing, dreaming, imagining goals,
A happy cheer,
Ronaldo's siu we hold dear!

Yusuf Sadek (6)
Canon Barnett Primary School, London

Australia

A beautiful view that I wake up to every morning, I jump out of bed to feed the animals, but all I see are Enchantimals.

U nder the sun, I'd love to help animals, but where are they? I need to find them today.

S hare the word, help the animals and make a community, but when they're not here there's no fam to see.

T ake the sick animals home and raise them until they're ready. Wild, but sometimes the wilderness is very mild.

R aise up a sick koala, then let it out in the wild so it can enjoy its life.

A dream I had when I was two: I had a dream to help the koalas do what they needed to.

L earn to help an animal, I'd rush downstairs and grab my bike, bare-footed ride to the wild and help the animals.

I didn't think this day would come but it looks like my koala business is now done.

A nd yes! I wake up and rush downstairs to find a room of grey sleeping bears.

Florence Mann (8)
Cobham Free School, Cobham

Girl On The Moon

One night, I was transported to a majestic dreamworld,
I found myself lying on the cold, hard ground,
Things like birds and books started flying around my injured head,
As they began to fade away,
Things like hot air balloons started picking me up from the ground,
I found myself floating all the way up to the moon,
Where there was a stack of books, saying, *'Read me, please'*,
Then I realised the moon was speaking,
The moon wanted me to sit there and read to him,
As I started reading the books,
The moon started to drift off to sleep,
The sun started rising and the moon started falling,
I got worried I was going to drift off into space,
Tonight had been very strange,
So I jumped...
I found myself back on a hot air balloon,
It was taking me back to where my house was,
I found myself standing at my front door,
Like nothing had happened,

My brother was still fast asleep, not in his usual place,
looking through my stuff,
I crawled back into my bed,
I wonder what will happen tomorrow in Dreamworld?

Audrey Stephens (9)
Cobham Free School, Cobham

Axolotl

A dream went flying in my head
A house which my auntie, uncle and cousins lived
I pulled out my xylophone to call my pet Lilly
I made an alarm for Lilly with my call
But nothing came
So I waited
Laughing going down the stairs
"Lilly, come here
It's all fun and games
Come here!" I said nervously
Down the stairs I went
I saw a pleasant sight
A fish tank with a purple axolotl
"A decorated tank," I shouted
"What I have is an axolotl
Where is Lilly?"
I went up the stairs happily
"I have an axolotl!"
I was lost when I went upstairs
And hugged my auntie, uncle and cousins
They lived greatly.

Maya Haluszczak (8)
Cobham Free School, Cobham

Once I Had A Dream

Once I had a dream
Nowhere I expected
In a place I've never been.
I was with my mum
In a dark and scary scene
Grateful that we weren't alone
But my sister and brother were gone.
Have I ever been more frightened?
I saw a policeman running down the street
I pulled my mum before she broke her core
We hid in our house for an hour more
Until we couldn't sit anymore for sure
I was as frozen as an igloo
As petrified as a tired little bunny
I closed my eyes and looked again
After that, I was as snuggled as a polar bear
Then I fell back to sleep in my small den
Today was almost as fun as a funfair
Then I was lost for words.

Umarah Choudhury (8)
Cobham Free School, Cobham

The Big Dream

There I was, drifting off and then... *poof!* I was in a new world.
Huh, huh, I was coming out of the changing room and into the Liverpool tunnel.
My heart was beating at 100mph and then I started to walk out.
Suddenly huge lights were beaming out at me
And millions of people in the crowd screaming, "*You'll never walk alone.*"
63 minutes in and there was a corner for Liverpool against Real Madrid.
Bam! A header from Banksy on his debut in the Champions League final.
Eh, that was the final whistle and I scored the winning goal!
But just when I ran to my teammates,
I suddenly woke up to my mum on a Wednesday morning at 7:15am.

Arthur Banks (8)
Cobham Free School, Cobham

A Brave Night

A s I drifted off to sleep, a galaxy of feelings
B anged in my head as the dreams popped up. I
R ushed away in the dark spooky woods.
A s the boulder came rolling at me, I was
V ery scared, as the boulder almost tripped me up.
E very bone in my body was shaking, as the boulder

N early made me as flat as a pancake as I quickly rushed for cover,
I hid in a cave, but there was something
G rowling, I thought it was a bear, but I was wrong, it was a
H yena! I rushed out of the cave and hid in a
T ight little den far away from the cave, but it was still in sight.

Amelia Murrle Milhac (9)
Cobham Free School, Cobham

I Woke Up In A Dream

I was wrapped up in my bed, all cosy and snug.
I looked over my toes and saw my bedroom rug.
I drifted to sleep,
Dreaming of cows and sheep.
All sorts of animals were in my head.
Luckily, I was home in my bed.

Poof went the dream of the cows and the sheep,
Then there was something more unique.
Drip, bang! I was in a different town.
Then, I realised I was upside down.

A world of adventure.
A world of risk.
Lots of things I wouldn't want to miss.
A world that's different;
A world where you walk on your hands, not feet.
My dream of holding a handstand's complete.

As I looked around, no one was there.
Apart from a baby hare.

Evangeline Scanlan (8)
Cobham Free School, Cobham

Dream World Full Of Surprises

I wake up in Dreamland, upside down
Wonderfully the village in the sky is as green as an emerald
The clouds are as fluffy as a kitten
Trees down below when hit with an axe, it makes a bang
Houses are made of cotton candy
Trees made of toffee and candy straws
Animals so cute, you can't help to touch them
The scary thing is the skeleton dungeon
It is the place you go when you have been bad
As you try to break in, the skeleton guard will stab you with a fine axe
It is made of blood and bones
Sometimes we go to war, and the skeleton army always wins.

Oscar Hodgetts (8)
Cobham Free School, Cobham

Fly To The Moon

S pace is my dream, I'm about to get on my rocket.
P urple and blue, it's a shiny rocket off I go.
A stronaut Elsie rockets into space.
C ities full of stars all around me are so beautiful.
E *cho echo echo* in my rocket ship, *whoosh, whoosh*, what a blast.

G azing at the stars, Venus and Mars.
I see beautiful patterns in the stars. Lots of people everywhere.
R ojo-Bobbit is hugging me as tight as he can.
L osing my mind in space tonight, *whoosh*, so much fun.

I love space.

Elsie Carter (9)
Cobham Free School, Cobham

Magic

My life stopped.
I was in a magical world, I could not believe this.
This was the journey I'd been waiting for.
As I walked on the soft marshmallow floor
I could feel my heart skip a beat.
I was so excited.
Grateful that I was in a calm place.
The glittering stars shone on my face.
It was there, a unicorn right in front of me.
It was magical, the best thing ever.
Crystal moon started to go down and then *boom*!
I was back in my bed.
And then I realised it was just a dream.

Alexa Rayment (9)
Cobham Free School, Cobham

Nightmare

As I drifted off to sleep
The moon rose and then the sun came down
I now was trapped in a world full of tunes
The fog swirled around my body
I had totally disappeared.

Suddenly, I appeared in a place of bones
Bones as cold as ice
On the riverbank by a sharp, grey
Sword covered with a drop of red blood
A gigantic bear had been beaten.

What type of beast could have hurt a creature this big?
His big eyes stared at me. *I don't think I will survive this.*
"Help! Help!" I cried.
All of a sudden, *plop*, I was in my bed.
Phew!

Oscar França (8)
Cobham Free School, Cobham

Chocolate, Mmm Yummy

W onderful chocolate.
I love chocolate, it is so so so delicious!
L indor is such a good chocolate, it is delicious.
L ove love love chocolate.
Y orkie Bars are so good because they melt in your mouth.

W ispas are so so bubbly.
O reo bars are so tasty.
N ero bars are amazing because they look so cool!
K it Kat bars are yummy as well.
A eros are really really really good as well because they look minty cool, taste great and are just amazing!

Genie Fraser (8)
Cobham Free School, Cobham

My Dreams

M y brain was exploding, oh no, was it 14th February 2029?
Y es, wait no! I'm not prepared, today it was...

D esigner Fashion Week!
R eally I was going to burst, I only had about 30 to 45 minutes
E ven though I thought I couldn't do it, I still had a spark of confidence
A fter a while, I was ready, okay, 20 minutes left, let's do this
M eanwhile, I had arrived, oh okay, this is a lot of people
S uper, yes I won, that was a lot of fun!

Amaris Crova (9)
Cobham Free School, Cobham

Nightmares

N ever in my life had I ever had a nightmare.
I look around in deep despair,
G leaming in the dark, I see a spooky clown,
H ow can this be happening? I have been found!
T o and fro I run, trying to shake the clown off, it is having fun!
M y heart is beating strongly like a drum,
A re there more? I hope not!
R ising carefully, some eerie eyes plot
E nd is near, I shut my eyes tight,
S uddenly, I am in my bed, no clowns in sight!

Michelle Botnarenco (9)
Cobham Free School, Cobham

Wonderfulness Poem

W hat is this land before my eyes?
O nly my favourite paradise,
N othing has prepared me for this,
D on't even know what this place is,
E verything is super weird,
R iding a car is a cow with a beard,
F inding random stuff everywhere,
U nder a table, a cup, and a guitar on a chair,
L ots of stuff are black and white,
N arwhals, elephants, trees and kites,
E verywhere there's only flowers,
S waying all about for hours,
S uper, the end!

Breandan-James O'Connell (9)
Cobham Free School, Cobham

Fire Dream

Waking up to a flame in my room,
Mum and Dad come rushing in.
"Mum, Dad, there's a flame in my room,
It's grown bigger and bigger. I don't know what to do."
People come rushing down the stairs, wailing in despair;
To see if they will have to evacuate.
People chatting like a hare
Running as fast as a cheetah,
With flames in their hair.
Fireballs coming from the air.
People running out of fuel, needing to really fuel
Wanting to get to safe land.
Watching people keep going; they can't though...

Harriet Druce (8)
Cobham Free School, Cobham

A Sugary Scare

One night when I was all snug in my bed,
Visions of sweeties danced in my head.
That night,
I took flight...

Everything went black.
Should I turn back?
I felt a tingle on my nose,
Then it went right down to my toes.

When I finally came around,
A rabbit appeared and came with a bound.
I scrambled to a tree, was it a spy?
I glanced up the tree, should I climb high?

To climb the tree was my decision,
But I would keep the rabbit in my vision.
When I touched the trunk, it was slimy and wet.
It was chocolate I bet.

Elizabeth Cooper (8)
Cobham Free School, Cobham

My Crazy Dream

I was in my bed all snuggly and warm.
But I knew that outside there was a storm.

Finally, after minutes of waiting, I fell asleep
But my head was saying,
"I'm going to scare you all through the night
With terror and *fright!*"

Before long, I forgot about the noises in my head.
I could still feel the blanket on my bed,
When suddenly...
Bash!
I could hear *creepy laughs.*

Darcey Dwyer (8)
Cobham Free School, Cobham

Dreamer

D own I went to a land of strange things, a flying sandwich with legs?
R ound and round went the trees, then *bang*, I was upside down.
E verywhere I went, birds were sitting and chickens were flying.
A unicorn with a dragon's body, a dragon with a unicorn's body and a cat with a sandwich head!
M aybe I was getting dizzy.
S oon I got used to it but then went back to my bedroom.

Marlie Scianna (8)
Cobham Free School, Cobham

Sleep

S lowly drifting away
L illy had a dream
E very night she had one
E very night she had the same one
P eople thought it was crazy but Lilly was just lazy.

T he next morning she fell asleep
I t turned out she was thinking of sheep
"**G** o away," she said in her dreams
H er brother peered in,
T hen he said it was just weird.

Grace Mickleburgh (8)
Cobham Free School, Cobham

Astro Diary

"**A** ll of this could be for nothing," I say to my partner,
"**S** oon we could be heroes or not."
 T his is the scariest part of my life!
 R ight then, we are blasting off 5, 4, 3, 2, 1,
 O n that very moment, we are blasting off,
 N ow we break the atmosphere,
 A ll is working itself out,
 U nder the moon, we lie,
 T he dark we see.

Michael Lancaster (8)
Cobham Free School, Cobham

Nightmares

N oisy branches watching over me
I thought it was snow but I was really wrong
G lowing in the middle of the woods, it must be a thought
H orrible pictures chasing me
T errifying things chasing from behind
M adness tearing my head
A lthough it must be a dream
R ustling under me
E very minute
S even thirty, I was in my town.

Haris Ali Khan (8)
Cobham Free School, Cobham

Dreamworld

D ashing across the football pitch,
R un through the football ditch,
E very year play in New York,
A nd crush them until they play more.
M atch starts, everyone yelling,
W in the match, everyone standing,
O ver the goal, the ball goes,
R ush to the ball, in the goal it goes,
L ineman running up and down,
D irect free kick, they're going down.

Eme Buckle (9)
Cobham Free School, Cobham

Lifetime

L ovely walk to the beach,
I nteresting creatures scattered around me.
F un swim and *boom* goes the waves in the sea.
E normous sandcastle with a flag on top,
T iny crabs tickling my toes.
I could feel the breeze in my hair,
M aking me an amazing mermaid in the sand.
E xciting day at the beach!

Molly McBride (8)
Cobham Free School, Cobham

The Best Football Players

Alisson is good at diving and stopping the ball,
Messi is good at vision, his amazing passing and is the best playmaker,
Neymar Jr is really talented and really good at skills and freekicks,
Ødegaard is good at passing, speed, shooting and freekicks,
Ronaldo is good at shooting, passing, freekicks, is really talented and he is the best.

Vincent Bashford (8)
Cobham Free School, Cobham

Dreaming

D ark, dark in the night,
R apid trees dancing with a fright,
E eek! Eeek! Mummy, I'm scared!
A nnoyed parents who haven't really cared,
M y gosh, where has she gone?
I think she has had the bear one!
N ight night, now don't you peek,
G o, go, go to sleep.

Hamish McAllister (8)
Cobham Free School, Cobham

Cars On Mars

C ars on Mars,
A s fast as Usain Bolt.
R ange Rovers passing by,
S uzukis as they zoom.

O ff-road cars flinging through the dust,
N issans passing me.

M ercedes Benz. Oh what fun!
A lpha Romeo just round the track.
R oar goes the Rolls Royce.
S uper Shelbys pass.

Amber Rayment (9)
Cobham Free School, Cobham

Nightmare

N othing was there,
I don't understand,
G urgling noises,
H owling noises,
T hundering noises,
M ost mysterious
A nd it was the scariest thing ever,
R unning downstairs terrified as can be,
E erie green eyes staring at me.

Jake Palmer (8)
Cobham Free School, Cobham

Gaming

G ames are good because you can play Fortnite.
A nd all of you play all night.
M ysterious me running through nobody's sight.
I 'm in the open doing something that can't be right.
N oisy me playing in a tree.
G oat simulator taking all the knights.

George Stevens (8)
Cobham Free School, Cobham

Australia

I went to my cousins'
On an aeroplane
Bang, crash went the luggage
My cousins burn in hot sun
Whilst I freeze on the plane
Koalas climbed from tree to tree
On arrival, greeted by my cousins waving
Travelling to their house
Looking out the window, birds flying.

Farah Mallindine (8)
Cobham Free School, Cobham

Night

N ever in my life have I seen a nightmare.
I was sleeping outside and it was a shining nightmare in my head.
G lancing through the night I began to shudder in fear.
H owever I saw a bright star and that made me feel special.
T hat night I loved the dark.

Mimi Barker-Dickson (8)
Cobham Free School, Cobham

Believe

When you believe, anything could happen
You could even drive a bus all the way to Saturn
Dreams will come true
When you bring magic along with you
So please take my advice
It might make you feel quite nice
So thank you for listening to me
I hope you enjoyed my poetry.

Elise Field-Rocks (8)
Cobham Free School, Cobham

Smile

S omewhere over the rainbow far, far away
M y brothers and I were having a play
I t was all nice and quiet until one strange noise started calling my name
L uckily, it was just my head being lame
E very skip, every hop and jump led right to my bed...

Gracie Parfitt (9)
Cobham Free School, Cobham

Mystery Of Bunny

B eautiful hair, cuddly cloud, soft fur, cute nose,
U nique, carrots, strawberries, dill, coriander,
N ibbling, jumping, stealing treats, wood toys,
N aughty, pee and poo in water.
Y ou will love them, sometimes and they are still very cute.

Bella Barker-Dickson (8)
Cobham Free School, Cobham

SpongeBob Fun

Soon I was in the world of SpongeBob.
Patrick was eating at Squidward's house.
Nobody was at the Krusty Krab.
Gary was at the park eating a Krabby Patty
Because SpongeBob made it.
One day I went to Patrick's house
Because it was fun.

Jude Monaco-Houghton (9)
Cobham Free School, Cobham

Cars Will Be Cars

Racing through my brain
A Caterham 7
But in the nearby
EV Heaven
A Tesla Roadster
They fancy a drag race
Until a BMW I8 breaks down
And got rid
Then it was taken to a motor show
But on the bid everyone said no.

Illy Alushi (8)
Cobham Free School, Cobham

Yes Day

Y elling children down the stairs
E lephants flowing like the air
S tinging bees in the trees

D ancing branches in the breeze
A ll the family feels so free
Y apping dogs playing with me.

Jess Harman (8)
Cobham Free School, Cobham

My Dream

Last night, I woke up with a scream,
Which made me get into a flap.
Because I thought they were coming to kidnap… me!

Then I realised it was just a dream
And I went back to sleep
To dreams of scones and cream.

Abigail Walker (9)
Cobham Free School, Cobham

World Cup

D efending the goal for my team,
R ussia was trying to score,
E veryone was cheering! "Harry, Harry."
A mid the pressure, my heart started beating
M y country needed me to win.

Harry McKenna (9)
Cobham Free School, Cobham

My Dreams

- **D** aring to jump and twirl upside down.
- **R** emembering my routine.
- **E** very step and leap.
- **A** high kick and front flip.
- **M** y dream of a gold.
- **S** tanding on the podium. Win a medal. Glowing bright.

Amelia Butler (9)
Cobham Free School, Cobham

My Basketball Matches

D *unk!* I've scored a three.
R oaring were the crowd, "Logan!"
E veryone was screaming my name
A hero is here!
M y famous medals tangle round my neck.

Logan Simpson (8)
Cobham Free School, Cobham

My Dreams

D ancing on the stage, singing like a lark
R afferty is a star
E veryone cheering like a dolphin
A miracle I knew I was a star
M y auntie thought I would go far!

Rafferty Liguorish (9)
Cobham Free School, Cobham

Time Travel

I time travel in my dreams,
I time travel in my head,
It sometimes feels like I time travel in real life
Usually, I end up in bed.

When I time travel in my head,
I end up in space,
Jumping planet to planet,
Then I'm on the moon in an astronaut suit.

When I time travel in my dreams,
There's a big, scary spider lurking in the house
Is it in the bath?
Splosh!
Is it in the bedroom snuggled up in bed?
Is it on the sofa watching TV?

When I time travel in real life,
I play in goal with all my friends up the pitch,
Anyone could come out of nowhere,
Then I'm on a big pitch playing for the Lionesses.

You see, dreams do come true.

Olivia Parry (10)
Gawber Primary School, Barnsley

My Dream About Football

I want to be a footballer
And score lots of goals.
No one would ever stop me because they'd be too slow.

I want to be a footballer
And be in the net.
I wouldn't let any goals in because I am the best.

I want to be a footballer,
I want to be a defender.
Then I would run and kick the ball from between people's legs
And I would run and score in the goal. *Bang!*
Then I'd be the best.

Now I am all grown up and in the World Cup.
Dreams do come true,
You just have to believe in you!

Emily Brotherton (10)
Gawber Primary School, Barnsley

The Real Santa

Yo, ho, ho,
We're ready to go,
To visit the real Santa.

We made this song,
As we sang along.
And this is how it went!

Yo, ho, ho,
We're ready to go,
To visit the real Santa.

I heard a whoosh,
So I had a look.
And a glimmer caught my eye.

It was Santa,
In his sleigh,
Eating a mince pie.

I waved at him,
And he waved back.
My heart full of delight.

So we made this song,
As we sang along.
And this is how it went!

Yo, ho, ho,
We're ready to go
Visit the real Santa.

Max Hill (10)
Gawber Primary School, Barnsley

Eye On The Ball

I'll keep my eye fixed on the ball
Whenever I play,
Whenever I fall.
I challenge the defence, speed up the field
To make opportunities real.
I'll get back up,
If I fall.
Never go down,
Never go around.
Never quit,
Never go to the pit.
If football's your thing,
Have a go.
No one will stop you,
No one will block you.
Keep your head high,
It's your time to shine.
Doesn't matter, boy or girl.
Be tall, be cool, be in time, be in line.
Have a dream tonight!

Jaiden-mai Skelley (10)
Gawber Primary School, Barnsley

Aliens

I wonder if there are aliens
And if they're experts
At flying around their planet
While eating a few peas?

If aliens are real
Maybe they are nice
They might even like things
That we humans like.

Maybe they are evil
And they'll want to go to war
They might have big weapons
Like laser guns and more.

Jacob Thistlewood (9)
Gawber Primary School, Barnsley

I Want To Be A Scuba Diver

I want to be a scuba diver
I want to be a scuba diver!
Swim with all the fish
The rolling waves would be my home
I'll splash around all day.

My house will be a clam
It's as quiet as a mouse
Some creatures may pounce
Like sharks and killer whales!

Some creatures move an inch.
Warning, crabs may pinch.
This is my home, I love every inch!

Erin Maunsell (9)
Gawber Primary School, Barnsley

Candy Land

Way up high above the clouds
Lies a land
A land as beautiful as crystals
A land of wonder and joy
And a land of candy!

Candy big
Candy small
Candy out of this world

But with one thing in common
They're all delicious!

The houses are made of gingerbread
With delicious squirty cream
But I know it's just a dream!

Charlotte Brayford (9)
Gawber Primary School, Barnsley

Eleven Things I Found In A Wizard's Pocket

A spooky night
A droopy cauldron
A splash of water
A human-sized cat that can't stay still
A wizard's hat
A lizard that eats children if they don't eat their vegetables
A magic spell book
A purple cauldron
A bucket of stars
A Mars bar
And don't forget the giant elephant!

Ava Woodhead (10)
Gawber Primary School, Barnsley

Tortoise

A tortoise is very cute.
A tortoise is very sweet.
Even if you annoy him,
He'd not bite,
He'd rather just retreat.

He doesn't want to play,
He doesn't want to come out!
He just wants to be left alone,
All day...

Seb Crossfield (9)
Gawber Primary School, Barnsley

I Want To Be A Footballer

I want to be a footballer
And score every shot
Be applauded by the crowd
And make my country proud
Win the La Liga, Premier League too
Win the World Cup for my country
I dream I'll be the best too!

Jenson Wilde (9)
Gawber Primary School, Barnsley

Space

Stars as bright as a million lightbulbs
And planets covered in colour.
Solar rays, black holes and moons
All things you can't defuse.
Planets like Jupiter and Mars
The Milky Way and millions of stars.

Henry Hays (10)
Gawber Primary School, Barnsley

I Want To Be A Goalkeeper

I want to be a goalkeeper,
And no one can stop me,
So I'm in the nets,
And I leap like a rabbit,
And save every shot
And win the World Cup!

George Bentley (9)
Gawber Primary School, Barnsley

Our Dreams

In dreams, we soar on wings of pure delight.
You and me will be standing at midnight.
Imagination takes us to great heights,
When the sun is gleaming and is so bright.

We dream of castles, dragons and magic.
People will think that this will end tragic.
Our minds are endless and never static,
When we don't sleep we will feel erratic.

In sleep's embrace, a world of wonders teem,
When twilight falls and stars begin to gleam.
Hopes and fears intertwine and entwine,
Dreams whisper secrets, so calm, so divine.

So close your eyes and let your dream take flight,
For in your dreams, you'll find your shining light.

Sonam Bansal (11)
Heath Park School, Wolverhampton

Space Dreams!

I'm flying up high
In the night sky,
Thinking of a dream
That can be seen.
Stars of royalty,
Making everything about reality.

Getting lost in a sphere
Can make us clear
To disappear
Building a chandelier
So all kinds of creatures can cheer
Magical veins
Going through the witch's cane.

Side by side
Or miles apart
You will have one star
Connected by a heart.

Chantelle Sliwa (11)
Heath Park School, Wolverhampton

Under The Moonlight

Crippled leaves swayed gently from left to right,
Rain hurled down in the eerie night.
The ripples of the water cleansed the silence,
A light shone exquisitely bright.
A pathway towards a wonderland,
The pristine water reflected towards it.
Droplets of water made the sound of soothing music
With the moonlight slowly descending,
Soothing music was put to a stop,
And rain held its breath.

Jana Abdullah (12)
Heath Park School, Wolverhampton

In My Dreams...

In my dreams, I can see,
Beautiful colours flying past me.
In my dreams, I can smell,
Mesmerising scents that ring a bell.
In my dreams, I can hear,
The jaw-dropping sounds of a deer.
In my dreams, I can taste,
Delicious foods that won't go to waste.
In my dreams, I can feel,
Amazing things that don't feel real.

Ara Amedi (12)
Heath Park School, Wolverhampton

Glaciers

As the archaic thick glacier melted at my feet
All I could feel was guilt
As I knew this was our bidding.
That this once strong, tall being
Was now Mother Nature's tears.
This isn't over,
It's far from it.

Henry Neale (12)
Heath Park School, Wolverhampton

Have You Ever Had A Dream?

Have you ever had a dream where you're flying?
I imagine that it is so satisfying!
Have you ever had a dream where you climb so high,
On a mountain made of ice cream that goes up to the sky?

Have you ever had a dream where you're driving a racecar,
That drives faster than a shooting star?
Have you ever had a dream where you're so tall,
You definitely wouldn't want to fall?

Have you ever had a dream where you have a pot of money,
Or a bath full of sticky honey?
Have you ever had a dream where you hop onto a ship,
That can go around the world in just one trip?

Have you ever had a dream where you go to space,
To try and save the entire human race?
Have you ever had a dream where you go on a train,
It's so much fun that I can't even explain.

Next time you go to bed and close your eyes,
You'll be in for a big surprise!
Dreams are only as big as your own imagination,
Who knows what will be your next creation?

Parker Christensen (9)
Ironville And Codnor Park Primary School, Nottingham

Ballin' Dreams

B lissfully, I close my eyes and fall to sleep
A ggressively, I grab the ball and leap
L oudly, the crowd cheers as I slam dunk
L ooking around, my heart sunk
I can't believe we're five minutes away
N ow they just stole the ball they'll pay

D ribbling the ball, they lose grip
R acing to gain control, they slip
E agerly, I grab the ball
A s I shoot and win the game, the referee calls
M y mum shouts as I awaken
S hooting out of my bed, it's time for bacon.

Elijah Coope (11)
Ironville And Codnor Park Primary School, Nottingham

A Dream

Once upon a time, I had a luxury dream,
When my bed was made of whipped cream,
And our kitchen full of amazing snacks,
Also a counter made of flapjacks!

I looked outside at the garden shed,
And it was made of gingerbread,
Then I saw a portal tall and thin,
I was also stuck right next to the bin.

So in the portal, I did climb,
For an adventure ahead of time,
Whirling and whizzing around I go,
Where will I stop? I don't know.

And then right at the very end,
I got woken up by a friend,
I really wanted to see what happened next,
However, who knows? I could have been vexed.

Rhys Finney (10)
Ironville And Codnor Park Primary School, Nottingham

Different Worlds

In a dream, there are so many possibilities
Like being trapped in an alien facility
Being forced to reveal everything in your memory
Trapped in a jail for more than a century

Or being able to fly across the world
Being so stretchy that your arms curl
Have super strength, lifting mountains
Be like a fish, breathe even when you're swimming in a fountain

Be a dog, a pig, or any more
Be the last man standing in a war
In a dream you can do anything you want
But when you wake up, you just can't.

Freddie Hendy (9)
Ironville And Codnor Park Primary School, Nottingham

Once Upon A Dream

My house was made of chocolate bars,
With marshmallow windows,
Shiny edible chairs with chocolate on top,
With a massive gingerbread door.

Live chocolate bunnies hopping around
The carrot cake trees swaying and dancing
A vanilla ice cream tower melting and making a pool
The fluffy clouds taste just like cotton candy.

Live gingerbread men swayed and twirled in a maze
You could see them with just one gaze.
The gingerbread man ran as fast as he could,
You can't catch me I'm the gingerbread man!

Suddenly the dream ended.

Alexis-Leigh Hale (11)
Ironville And Codnor Park Primary School, Nottingham

Once I Had A Dream

My sofa is cotton candy,
My friend is called Andy.
My bed is cake
And I live over a lake.

My house is on a cloud,
And it is not loud.
I can fly
And touch the sky.

I don't lie,
I cannot die.
Maybe you can try?

I look next door
And there's a dance floor.
I start dancing,
A horse is prancing.

I look again
And see a chocolate factory,
Go inside
And see a chocolate gallery.

There is a beam
And that's my dream.

Bobby Squares (9)
Ironville And Codnor Park Primary School, Nottingham

Dream, Dream, Dream

Once upon a dream,
I dream to play on a professional women's team.
"Proctor, Proctor, Proctor," I can hear it now.
Run, run, run, I can score, *pow!*

No one knows how hard I try.
Boys say I'm bad, so I try not to cry.
I have a dream to play in the women's World Cup.
And I have my team lift me up, up, up.

Changing into the women's kit.
After the match at Wembley Stadium, I sit
Swapping shirts and taking pics.
After the game, changing my boots for my designer kicks.

Ava-Grace Proctor (11)
Ironville And Codnor Park Primary School, Nottingham

Life Is But A Dream

Have you ever had a dream
Where your house is made of ice cream?
What if you had a cotton candy floor
And maybe even a chocolate door?
Close your eyes
Let your imagination fly away
See a picture
Of where you wish to be one day
Hold on tight and nurture it
But allow it room to grow
When you reach your dream
Open your hand and let it go.

Lacie-Anne Robinson (11)
Ironville And Codnor Park Primary School, Nottingham

Football Dreams

Being a footballer is my dream
I love playing with my team
Passing around and scoring goals
Running around into poles
Mum and Dad cheering me on
I think this is where I belong
Muddy boots and tired legs
I hope I don't get megged.

Kaeden Akers (10)
Ironville And Codnor Park Primary School, Nottingham

A Football Dream

I came to play football in a team
To play for Nottingham Forest is my dream
To suddenly be praised
Soon my coach will be amazed
With my bright yellow boot
I went and did a shoot
"Goal!" I shouted, it went in
Afterwards, I had a party with my kin.

Darcie Squires (10)
Ironville And Codnor Park Primary School, Nottingham

Once Upon A Path

A path so long
With weird and wacky, soft and sweet
Random things you can eat.
First on the path, a peculiar house
With twenty doors and twenty windows
Colourful lights flash here and there
Monkeys swing up and down
Dropping lollipops on the ground.
Now this house - this house indeed,
Stood on the highest hill where butterflies walk and cats fly
Everything is weird and has googly eyes.

Next on the path, McDonald's burgers, fries galore,
Mice sit around on cheesy pillows with gumdrop cocktails and spaghetti wheels.

Last on the path,
Two pelicans having a laugh,
One called Pete, one called Cath,
And under their wing was a little baby cat.
All cuddled up in a little ball fast asleep,
Dreaming of the very same path you are reading.

Ruby Watts (10)
New Road Primary School, Sowerby Bridge

I Have A Dream

I have a dream to live in a house,
With a door made out of a sugar mouse.
With a chocolate lane,
And windows made out of candy canes,
And a roof made out of milk chocolate.

In the back garden, there is a candyfloss poodle,
Jelly snake, and a gummy bear.
The flowers are made out of M&M's,
And the grass is made out of liquorice laces.

Inside is a bed made out of jelly,
And at the side of the bed is a table,
Made out of dark chocolate.

In the kitchen there is
An oven made out of gobstoppers.
The table is made out of a selection box,
And the two chairs are made out of marshmallows.

In the living room there is a TV made out of a Wispa,
The sofa is made out of liquorice
And the pillows are made out of marshmallows.

Evie Potts (10)
New Road Primary School, Sowerby Bridge

The Dream Factory

With a flick of a switch and a pull of a lever,
A turning of cogs, a cycle that goes on forever.

Dreams are spun and weaved,
Rainbow colours,
Dreams of lovers,
Fairies and others dancing on starlit worlds.

Nightmares are forged and shaped,
Ink black smoke,
Otherworldly features,
Bloodthirsty creatures prowling under a starless sky.

Dreams are stored and stashed,
Shining like silver in golden ribbon-wrapped jars,
Nightmares are locked and kept,
In metal cages where it's like a prison behind bars.

When night finally makes its arrival,
The dreams are ready to go,
Poured onto everyone's pillows,
All around the globe.

Arabella Haleywood (11)
New Road Primary School, Sowerby Bridge

Sweet Dreams

In my dream world we have candy cane trees,
With cookie-dough houses, unlocked with chocolate keys.
There are lots of dogs living everywhere,
With marshmallow faces and cotton candy hair.

In this world, we have unlimited food,
No one goes hungry, everyone is in a good mood.
There is a gingerbread palace where the royals are,
Parked outside in their fancy sugar-dough car.

There are cupcakes as door handles, topped with whipped cream,
I wish this was real, this is my dream.

Daisy Brocklehurst (10)
New Road Primary School, Sowerby Bridge

My Fluffy Cloud

In my dream world, I live on a fluffy cloud,
My house is made of cotton and floats above the ground.
My roof tiles are pillows,
And jumping around are living jellos.

It's a beautiful world of imagination,
The rainbows are sweets of my creation.
The chair is a teddy,
That is eating spaghetti.

In my dream world, I have grapes that are blue,
And lemons that are pink.
The table has fur painted with ink.
When you look at the cloud, you choose what you see.
You might see a big city or a broccoli tree.

Eliza Siwerska (10)
New Road Primary School, Sowerby Bridge

Nightmares Take Over!

In this lava land dreams are trapped in cages above a red-hot river.
Trees filled with skulls that will give you a shiver.
Memorable nightmares in a globe.
But watch out for the lightning strobe.
Dreams locked up with no freedom,
Waiting to be unlocked by the demon.

Fire rabbits destroying jolly dreams.
Their appetites satisfied by their screams!
Demons smelling the strange flowers,
Whilst the others are using their godly powers.

Poppy Prescott (11)
New Road Primary School, Sowerby Bridge

Nightfall

On this land, we cannot leave,
We are stuck in the dreams of those who believe.
Nightmares roam around and free,
While we're all stuck sobbing our last plea.
When the sun comes up, they are safe and sound,
But when the moon rises, we bury their dreams underground.
Sadness swells all over their faces,
While the nightmares carry on their cases.
Showing everyone something new,
It finally comes to meet you too...

Iris Parkinson (11)
New Road Primary School, Sowerby Bridge

A Tasty Dream

Our dream world is made of food - how tasty,
When everything's food you can have a nice pastry.
There are over 100 pizza places in all of the land,
It is time to try this really cool new brand.
A marshmallow blizzard happens once a week,
With chocolate rain that is easy to eat.
There are pancake lilypads in the chocolate river,
There is ice cream cold enough to make you shiver.

Finn Stephenson (10)
New Road Primary School, Sowerby Bridge

Dream World

In my dream world the houses are made of chocolate,
The clouds are cotton candy, how funny,
Everything is fine and jolly.

Trees so tall they touch the sky,
Grab yourself an apple pie,
Do not cry,
Grass so tall, we do not die.

Toffee rivers everywhere,
Get yourself a flump,
Don't get into a grump,
In this land, you can not leave.

Lainy Bolton (11)
New Road Primary School, Sowerby Bridge

Tasty Sweet World

In my dream world, you can find cotton candy parks
Parts of the park are strawberry, others bubblegum, how yummy
You can find pictures of a guy with a strawberry tummy, how funny.

In my dream world, there are candy glass trees,
With the jelly bean bees
Oh, and I can not forget the brownie seas, how jolly
You can also find lolly brollies
Also your money is made out of marshmallow.

Maisie Smith (10)
New Road Primary School, Sowerby Bridge

Dream Garden

In our dream world, we have guinea pigs,
With candy canes that lead your way,
Cotton candy clouds roam the sky,
Do not cry, do not lie,
Houses made out of white chocolate, how crazy,
In this world, we are not lazy,
In the garden there are daisies,
In the garden, there are chocolate lanes,
Leading your way, made of candy land.

Lexi Churchward (10)
New Road Primary School, Sowerby Bridge

The Power Of Flick

In my dream world, we have infinite money
When you flick, you teleport anywhere
The people with infinite money can get a candy house
And when you flick two times food appears.
You can fly and can go in invisible and you can hold your breath forever.
No homework and only golden time and PE.

Jack Jackson (11)
New Road Primary School, Sowerby Bridge

What A Dream

My dream is that one day I will be able to breathe fire
And that Pokémon are real.
In my dream world, there will be no homework
And my hair stays neat and tidy all day.
I will be able to see my mum more
Dreams can't be dreams without love.

Lexie Quigley (11)
New Road Primary School, Sowerby Bridge

The House

I like in a house,
A very peculiar house,
Walls of Skittles,
Grass of chocolate,
Where the poodles play.

A rugby pitch,
Full of chocolate players,
A golden toilet,
Giant hornet, tree swing,
With extra sprinkles.

Mason Collier (11)
New Road Primary School, Sowerby Bridge

Once Upon A Dream

In my dream world,
I have unlimited Robux
That gives you good looks.
There are chocolate reindeer - how yummy,
Cotton candy dogs - how funny

Infinite money for all,
Bikes that go fast,
They leave bubbles at last.

Zac Woodyatt (10)
New Road Primary School, Sowerby Bridge

My Marvellous Dream

In my dream world, we have purple skies,
People have wings, not just flies.
You can go live in a Best Buy,
You can go to a rugby field and score a try.
Houses are made out of chocolate pie,
So much it could make you cry.

Lincoln Taylor (10)
New Road Primary School, Sowerby Bridge

Once Upon A Dream

In my dream world,
I have pillows made of lollies, how jolly.
Chocolate bushes full of holly, haha so funny.
M&M leaves slowly drift from the sky, I wonder why.
Windows made of candyfloss that do not cry.

Eva Taylor (11)
New Road Primary School, Sowerby Bridge

The Greatest Match

I was standing in the middle of the goal,
Waiting for the referee to blow the whistle,
If I saved this, I'd win and my country would win.
The roars of the crowd ringing in my ears,
My bottom lip quivered,
Adrenaline pumping through my veins,
My heart dropped as I heard the deciding whistle,
This was it, this was the goal or save that would change my life forever.
The opponent finally steps up to take the shot,
Before I knew it, I was in the air,
It was almost like slow motion.
My hand whacked the ball as I saw it go into the sidelines.
I had done it, I had just won the World Cup.
My teammates sprinted over to me as I burst into tears of happiness.

Henry Pepper (10)
Newington Community Primary School, Ramsgate

The Nightmare That Became A Dream

Once every night
Your mind takes flight
A dream is made
Only for your mind

Me and Katie walked back from school
It was a hot day
We wanted to swim in a pool
Crunch! Crunch! Crunch! The leaves went
We realised somebody was behind us

They had a spot with paws
A golden name label which said 'Harriet'

"I love sweets," a faint voice could be heard
It looked like they had a pet bird
Me and Katie ran faster than a cheetah
But we still got caught

I woke up in a van
It was hot, I needed a fan
Katie could not be seen

Even when I leaned
She was not there

Sadly it was just me
I was thirsty, I wanted some tea
It was lonely
So lonely it felt ghostly

I was dropped off in a wood
My friend Joe had some food
It seemed he was brought here
He didn't want to cheer

I found Katie asleep
She was in a deep sleep
The tree she was resting on was large
These conditions were harsh

Harriet was standing on a stage
She looked very brave
Paper was in her hands
The paper was a speech she held while she stands

Attention
I wanted to say thank you
Hostages listen
Well done Eve

Who was Eve?
Did Harriet have a secret up her sleeve?
Weird words came out of her mouth
And she was pointing south.

Jamie Ferguson (10)
Newington Community Primary School, Ramsgate

The Dark Room

N estled in my bed, resting my head.
I listen to my clock when it strikes 12 o'clock.
G ripping my cover tight, I have a fright. I wake to find that I am not in my bed.
H ow did I get here? Is this real or in my head?
T o find that I'm in a dark room with no light ahead.
M y heart beats fast to see something in the corner of the room.
A s I try to run away, I can not move. It feels like I'm standing in glue.
R eminding myself that this is not real. Wake up, wake up, wake up.
E yes open. To my relief, I'm in my room all snuggled in bed.
S leeping in my bed, no bad dreams lie ahead.

Mollie Simpson (10)
Newington Community Primary School, Ramsgate

The Fairytale Dream

Ready for bed, to rest for the night,
When I switch off my bedroom light.

Time to sleep, ready to explore,
To dream of creatures, magic or more?

I conjure up a luxurious horse,
Galloping in my dreams of course!

In the lovely clear moonlight,
I see that it is purest white.

I see a princess, her hair is blonde,
The horse and her have a good bond.

Behind her on her horse is a prince,
Deep in love, I am convinced.

I dream of being like her, in love,
But what are these creatures flying above?

Scaring people below in wagons,
I see fire-breathing dragons!

But as quick as night becomes day,
The gallant prince scares them away!

My mother calls me, it's very abrupt,
Then I realise it's time to wake up.

Ocean Perry (11)
Newington Community Primary School, Ramsgate

The Day I Became A Freak

I had a dream where I had powers
Maybe like growing flowers
But today was different and worse
It was almost like some sort of curse
It started off with radioactive water
I fell into it sort of
First I got pushed in
By someone called Lin
What got blurry was my vision
I got a terrible condition
I now look like a freak
Lin is the one I seek
I now crave for meat
And I grew giant feet
Then I developed some sort of skill
One that let me heal
And suddenly I flew up
And whoever I touched blew up
Then I found Lin, I shoved her in a bin
She will pay
She won't live another day.

Henry Harmes (10)
Newington Community Primary School, Ramsgate

Dreams In A Puddle

Down in the dungeon,
A misty puddle awaits your return, you would say.
There, in the reflection,
Doom shall fade away.
At first glance, a dream visitor
There, as you take it
The ground opens down to the Earth's core.
A sight to see
A magical flute,
You found your glee.
Bubbles in the rainbow,
Whoosh, a flaming phoenix swoops by.
Myths like the Night Show
Centaurs, mermaids, dragons, all day
Ding! Dong! It's already dawn.
It's like time flies by! You wish to stay.
Pulled out the puddle
Today in bed
My mind's in a muddle!
And a hot chocolate in my hand.

April Bradshaw (10)
Newington Community Primary School, Ramsgate

My Dream

N othing has prepared me for the weird land I see,
I take a step forward, as nervous as I can be,
G lancing left and right, all I see is smoke,
H ow did I get here? I really hope this is a joke,
T *hud*, something moves, it's really creeping around,
M y worst fear is a spooky scary clown,
A manic grin spreads across its face,
R unning like a bolt, it starts to give chase,
E erie eyes glow, I close my own in dread,
S uddenly I wake to find it was a dream.

Bella Bull
Newington Community Primary School, Ramsgate

Seasons

December, January, February
This is when it comes!
That cold that jogs your memory!
Especially the numbness in your thumbs.

March, April, May
When flowers start to blossom,
Whilst the sun comes out to play
And the bees don't have a problem!

June, July, August
The best season of the year
I'm being truly honest
It's fun to jump off the pier.

September, October, November
The leaves begin to brown
Always try to remember,
To turn that frown upside down.

Freya Holt (10)
Newington Community Primary School, Ramsgate

Once Upon A Dream

Once upon a time,
A young girl went to bed,
And woke up in a land,
Where the sky was glowing rainbow,
And elegant dragons flew through the clouds.

Running on the ground, lots of majestic creatures,
Like unicorns, pegasuses and glow worms.

The young girl looked next to her,
To see a unicorn,
Bent down for her to climb on,
Then she climbed on and started galloping,
"Woo hoo!" bellowed the girl.

At that moment, everything around her
Was fading away,
In a rainbow tornado,
And she woke up in her bed.

Millie Lambert-Robins (11)
Newington Community Primary School, Ramsgate

The Feelings That Keep Me Up At Night

What is time?
Do we know?
What is an hour of a day?
Twenty-four there is today.

Time has gone so fast.
I was once a baby
And now I am a lady.
I have to check the time, time and time again.
And there I am a little bit older.

The time has come for me to start
My new chapter.
Secondary school, that's what's waiting for me.
Time to look forward and not behind.
But still, I stand still, thinking,
Looking at time
Sixty minutes an hour,
Twenty-four hours a day
A week passes in a lifetime.

Taylia Baker (11)
Newington Community Primary School, Ramsgate

Nightmare

N o one was around me, I was in a haunted mansion!
I found the scariest thing ever!
G hosts and aliens, I ran to find somewhere to
H ide. The aliens had black eyes
T hat looked like black holes. The ghosts were pale,
M ansion was very big so I could make
A run for it, but it was going to be hard.
R an as quick as a flash through the
E ntrance. I made it, I decided to go home.

Charlie Cox (11)
Newington Community Primary School, Ramsgate

Beach Day

The sun is dazzling. Ow! That's hot,
Beware of the sand, it's like a boiling pot,
Diving into the water with fish at your feet,
Or sitting on your pink inflatable seat,
Focus on the ball as it bounces fast,
Quick, quick, quick, don't let it get past,
Snorkelling under that deep blue sea,
Seeing all of the fish swimming free,
Turtles, starfish, dolphins too,
I even see an old telephone booth!

Sofia-Dolce Adams (11)
Newington Community Primary School, Ramsgate

My Mysterious Dream

Oh mysterious dream that appeared in my head,
Will you show me the future that lies ahead?
I think of you and where you might be,
Are you real or just a fantasy?
Through light and darkness you are to me,
The beautifulness of a mystery,
I search and search but I cannot find,
That thing from you that I call mine,
I look in the mirror but what do I see?
The reflection of a person that could be... me!

Kirsten Valentina Tschirschky-Okoro (11)
Newington Community Primary School, Ramsgate

The Night Of Bad Dreams

Trapped in a meadow, you hear no sound.
But there are demons and monsters all around.
You think you're safe, but is it true?
Something reaches and grabs you.
Down you go, deep into the shadows,
Will you survive? Nobody knows.
Your eyes snap awake, there's no time to grin,
Check your body, limb by limb.
There's nothing wrong, it's all okay.
You fall asleep, hoping it stays that way.

Alfy Allen (11)
Newington Community Primary School, Ramsgate

My Pet Dinosaur

I have a dinosaur whose name is Bob.
He is blue and green and a bit of a slob.
We eat pizza and chips and ice cream for dessert.
Which can make my Bob go a bit berserk.
When we go out, everyone screams.
So we zoom through the sky like a rocket machine.
If Bob gets silly, he poops on a car.
Yes, my dinosaur is really bizarre.
When we get home, we go to bed.
All snuggled up and drifting ahead.

Max Teyn (11)
Newington Community Primary School, Ramsgate

Neverland

N othing has prepared me for this amazing land
E verybody is happy not sad
V ariety of dreams
E veryone will turn into trees
R unning away from evil devils
L ate nights with different levels
A lways perfect no matter what
N o more hiding in a hut
D reams are always different either happy or sad, don't worry you're not the only one.

Aziell Ong (11)
Newington Community Primary School, Ramsgate

Football Dream

F orever I've dreamed of becoming a pro
O f hearing the crowd cheer as I go for the goal
O nwards I push as I weave through players
T hey say with the ball I'm a skilful operator
B alancing my body as I move with the ball
A ll my focus is on the goal
L ooking from the stalls, my family watch enthralled
L oyal to the sport, I give it my all.

Theo Usman (11)
Newington Community Primary School, Ramsgate

Dream Big

When I close my eyes to sleep,
These weird things in my mind begin to creep,
Kittens with mittens and dogs with boots,
Lollipops for trees with gigantic fruits,
Goats with coats,
Rabbits with ties,
Where a lie is a truth and a truth is a lie,
What is this magical wonderland?
It is certainly the least of bland,
Oh why, oh why,
When I open my eyes,
The enchanting fantasy dies?

Holly-Anne Vine (10)
Newington Community Primary School, Ramsgate

The Magic Will Never End

My dream is to go to Harry Potter World,
Where the magic never ends.
To see the props, wands and beyond
To see the books and films I love come to life
With my family of four, we pretend to be wizards galore.
To dragons and witches, we will experience it all.
I'll be happy and excited and have fun while teasing
My brother with my magic wand.
I'll go to bed tonight and dream of the wonders of it all.

Abigail Smith (10)
Newington Community Primary School, Ramsgate

The Flying Dogs

Once, I had a dream that all dogs could fly,
They sprouted puppy wings and took to the sky,
Their owners held on to their leads so tight that
Some of the pooches looked like kites,
Just as I was about to let my own dog go,
I felt something wet on the end of my nose,
I opened my eyes to the lick from my pup,
It was all just a dream and time to get up!

Max Booker (10)
Newington Community Primary School, Ramsgate

A Tale Of Snakes

A snake was following me,
Up into a forbidden tree,
I almost couldn't breathe,
At the sight of what I saw.

Poison fangs had bitten me,
As I started to scream,
What I saw I couldn't believe,
The snake was eating ice cream.

The snake had a team,
All ready to bite me,
Then I woke up with a scream,
Before I realised it was all a dream.

Scarlett (11)
Newington Community Primary School, Ramsgate

Dancer

D ancing around with magical toes,
A ll around up and down like a yo-yo,
N ow I've started I never want to stop,
C an't imagine doing anything else so magical,
E ntertaining family and turn to a celebrity,
R ound and round you turn and float.

Daisy Lilley (11)
Newington Community Primary School, Ramsgate

Tenerife

T ravelling on a plane
E lla my sister is being a pain
N ight sky shines so bright
E arly morning sun is so light
R acing down the slides at Siam Park
I n the dark
F un activities to learn
E veryone getting sunburn.

Olivia Cameron (10)
Newington Community Primary School, Ramsgate

Unicorns

U nicorn's hair can be any colour you want
N eighing all day in the sun
I n the night mischief begins
C limbing mountains while eating green grass
O n the clouds, we lie
R eady for a nap
N ow we start it all over again.

Poppy Lowe (10)
Newington Community Primary School, Ramsgate

Unicorns

Up, up... high in the sky,
(Not that you'll see them - they're really shy!)
Imagining touching their mesmerising horns,
But cautiously - I must warn
Because once you're in its sight,
It will rear back, then take flight,
Never to be seen again...

Lillie Gould (11)
Newington Community Primary School, Ramsgate

Dreams

D o as you wish,
R eminiscing the past and wishing you were there,
E xciting wishes come true,
A mazing things can happen,
M emories that will last forever,
S ucceeding when I am dreaming.

James Smith (10)
Newington Community Primary School, Ramsgate

Bees

Bees are beautiful
Bees are clever
Bees are important
Bees buzzing everywhere
Flying in the summer air between the flowers and the trees
Having a rest upon the leaves
Creating a beautiful world for you and me.

Mason Chadd (10)
Newington Community Primary School, Ramsgate

The Footballer

I take the pass in
The crowded playground and
The ball's tamed by my foot
And goes where I will it to.
I take off slow,
Slide round the tackler's pass
And the skipping girl,
Dodge the watching teacher,
Whirl on my heel.

Michael Safronov (11)
Newington Community Primary School, Ramsgate

Candy Land

Am I awake or is this a dream?
I'm in a bath full of strawberries and whipped cream,
Sprinkles and cherries and sauce galore,
Leaves my belly wanting more,
There's candy canes everywhere,
And gummies and gummies that taste like pear,
Oh look, there's a slide lets go,
I hope I land in a pool of marshmallow,
There's jelly beans too,
Too many flavours to tell you,
Now I'm full, I hope to wake
Before I get the world's worst tummy ache.

Honey Allard (9)
Rackheath Primary School, Rackheath

Space Dream

In my dream, I lie down to see
Rockets and spaceships flying over me,
Meteors and shooting stars
Whizzing past like racing cars,
An astronaut gives me a wave,
I wonder if his name is Dave!
The aliens go *beep, beep, beep,*
They're going to wake me from my sleep,
All this noise from asteroids,
Outer space is full of voids,
The galaxy and Milky Way,
Keeps me dreaming until it's day,
I wake up happy with a beam,
Shouting, "Mum, Mum! I had a dream!"

Harrison Petts (10)
Rackheath Primary School, Rackheath

Zombie Apocalypse

In my dreams every night,
Clouds and zombies fight,
The clouds filled with,
Anger, anguish and rage,
Poured down with blood,
The zombies were terrified,
"Stop now, or else!" they shouted,
Suddenly, the clouds turned as red as if on fire,
Therefore the strong Hulk zombies,
Gathered weapons together and started throwing axes,
To the raw, dark red clouds above,
Suddenly, I woke up in my bed.

Connor Appleton (9)
Rackheath Primary School, Rackheath

Dreams

You can go anywhere,
Joy will come with you,
Butterflies soaring high,
Anything is possible here,
The sweet smell of honey is in the air,
Candy canes swaying like trees,
Gingerbread houses lined in a row,
Candyfloss clouds floating by,
Peaceful melodies are playing in the distance,
A happy place to stay for a while,
Stirring, tingling, gradually awakening.

Rachel Bryan (10)
Rackheath Primary School, Rackheath

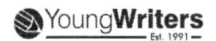

Dreamy Dreams

Dreams take you to places
You've never been before.
Dreams let you fly
Through a world of imagination.

Dreams are a release
From the world of reality.
Dreams let you live in a universe
Of your design.

Dreams are pure and beautiful,
Dreams are as special as you.

Isaac Rynn (10)
Rackheath Primary School, Rackheath

In My Dream

In my dream, I am a dancer, dancing and prancing around.
In my dream, I am a wizard, turning everyone into lizards.
In my dream, I am a pirate who wants to be a pilot.
In my dream, I am an athlete who only eats wheat.
In my dream, I am a scientist who is also an activist.
But in real life, I am just a child.

Emily Thoulass (10)
Rackheath Primary School, Rackheath

Thank You For My Friends

F un and caring
R eally good at sharing
I love our playground chats
E ating our crunchy snacks
N ever rude, always polite
D iscovering adventures with them is a delight
S haring their toys so eagerly.

Maxwell Sweatman (9)
Rackheath Primary School, Rackheath

Your Worst Nightmare

Thunder crashes, lightning strikes.
Ghostly noises echo through the night.
Surrounded by your worst nightmares.

A horde of tarantulas coming at you in front, scuttling closer.
A manic clown comes laughing to your left, a three-headed dog moves in barking, as you take a glance right.
Darkness flooding in behind, ear-splittingly loud fireworks crashing while coming in from above.

Just before you are devoured by a scruffy, hungry, three-headed dog a candy floss pink unicorn comes floating down on a bubble gum blue cloud.
Hopeful rainbows follow, chasing out the nightmares and letting the dreams flow.

The thunder was replaced by the thunderous applause from the happy spectators of the nearby magic show. The lightning replaced by rocking disco lights, and the ghostly noises replaced by fun merry music.

Around every corner you can find a good dream like cold, tasty ice cream or fluffy, cute puppies...

Welcome to your dreamland!

Imogen Eyres (10)
Sarum St Paul's CE (VA) Primary, Salisbury

My Baby Dragon

I dreamt of a baby dragon,
He was scaly and very blue.
He was being very naughty,
So I taught him a thing or two.

He was breathing fire everywhere,
That was a real shame,
So I tried to teach him
Where to shoot his flame.

I said, "Let's see if you can fly,"
So I sat on his back,
And in a flash,
We were flying through the sky.

We were flying really fast
Which was really, really thrilling,
So I thought I could train him
If he was quite willing.

I love my little dragon,
We really have a bond,
But if I'm going to train him properly,
I would need a magic wand.

My little baby dragon flew away,
My tears came out in screams,
But I knew I would see him again,
Asleep in my wonderful dreams.

Grace Bugden (9)
Sarum St Paul's CE (VA) Primary, Salisbury

Space Disco

A way to the stars
S aturn, Jupiter and Mars
T ravelling far away from home
R oaring off in our space rocket dome
O n past the twinkling stars we fly
N othing prepares us for the beautiful sky
A stronauts excited we danced in space
U p we groove in this intergalactic place
T wisting and turning sheets over my head
S uddenly I wake up back in bed!

Grace Parsons (10)
Sarum St Paul's CE (VA) Primary, Salisbury

Dreams

D own in the depths of the deep, blue sea
R ed dragons are hunting me, they have searched
E very nook and cranny but
A ll they found was an old granny
M other nature frowned upon this irresponsible behaviour
S uddenly, I woke up safe and sound at home with my brother Xaviour.

Evie Monington (10)
Sarum St Paul's CE (VA) Primary, Salisbury

The Figure In The Shadow

As I settle down to fall asleep,
I close my eyes, not daring to peep.
Drifting off, letting my mind control me, then get lost,
Into a horrible dream, oh no, she is coming, my life will come at a cost.
The fog appears, surrounding me as I let out a horrid scream,
Her nose is a shark's, her skin is slimy and green.
With a swoosh, then a cackle, she appears on her broom,
Her black cat, her bat, her voice goes boom.
She is a frightening murderer, she is a deadly killer,
If I get found, I am her dinner.
I cannot run, I cannot hide,
The taunting silhouette, the disturbing ride.
I look to the left, I see her standing there,
She has taken me into her lair.
She is a devil in disguise, evil, malicious,
And skilful - she is deadly, poisonous and vicious.
I am too late, I am now doomed,
Every night, she terrifies me and her voice booms.
I can't stare,
It is a very bad nightmare.

Darcey Doran (10)
Springwood Federation (Junior School), Waterlooville

Gingerbread Man

G ingerbread man coming out of the oven
I nches away from my mouth
N ibble, nibble, nibble, one last bite
G ulp, mmm, that was tasty
E rm, I wonder if I should make some more for my husband, he would love to have a treat
R eady to do something, let's start
B aking some treats, almost done
R eady, let's put the treats in ready for him, let's call
E dward. Come here, I've got some treats for you to try
A nd they're freshly baked, too.
D amn, these are *awesome*

M an, we should have these every day
A nd your cooking is so awesome
N obody could beat your cooking.

Kinley Speake (10)
Springwood Federation (Junior School), Waterlooville

The Malicious Witch

I was tucked in my bed,
Because I'm a sleepy head,
In the woods, there was a serial killer,
And I knew I was for dinner!

It was the dead of night,
And then I had a horrible sight!

She was a devil: menacing, sinful and malicious,
She was a scorpion: powerful, poisonous and vicious,
My legs were trembling,
Because I was remembering!
The nightmare I had last night,
It was such a bad fright,
I could not run, I could not hide,
And in a minute, she would be by my side.

I could hear sticks breaking,
But I was waking,
I knew it was nearly over,
Then I saw a four-leaf clover.

Now I knew it was my lucky day
I could say hip, hip hooray!
With a start, I sat up wide awake,
My body was trembling, it was a mistake!

Eli Humphris (10)
Springwood Federation (Junior School), Waterlooville

The Nightmare

At the stroke of midnight the moon rose high,
As the witch raced across the moonlit sky,
With teeth black as tar and manky straw-like hair,
Long bony fingers led me into her lair.
The cauldron was bubbling and shooting out silver stars,
Each one had a face all covered in scars,
On shelves round the room sat rats, cats and mice,
They smelt like death and were covered in lice.
The harridan prepared the oven to roast me alive,
I needed a place where I could safely hide,
In the corner stood an unusual casket,
I would have preferred a cosy warm basket.
At 6 o'clock the alarm went off,
As the witch was about to screw my head off.

Arabella Capell (10)
Springwood Federation (Junior School), Waterlooville

The Nightmare

Surrounded by the finger-like trees,
Covered in warts from her head to her knees.

Looking round to my left then my right,
She was there, ready to give me a fright.

As the moon rose in the night sky,
A small silhouette caught my eye.

There was a pool of victim's blood on the floor,
And then I heard a scream from behind the door.

She came out and saw me there,
Then she gave me the scariest glare.

She chased me through the forest and tore me apart,
And then she quickly ate my heart.

I woke up and screamed in terror,
And knew that dream would haunt me forever.

Marley Roberts (10)
Springwood Federation (Junior School), Waterlooville

The Witch Of My Nightmare

As I drifted off in my nice warm bed,
I snuggled close to my favourite ted.
I found myself near to a haunted tree,
I saw her silhouette, she taunted me.

Her bony fingers on her outstretched hand,
Her nose was a shark, I now understand,
I was screaming, panicking, full of dread,
I knew if I messed up I would be dead.

I peeped from my tree, no witch to be found,
She was behind me, I found myself bound.
Next thing I knew, she had torn out my heart,
I screamed so loud, I woke up with a start.

My body was shaking, I had finally hid,
She was my nightmare since I was a kid.

Medeea Sacuiu (9)
Springwood Federation (Junior School), Waterlooville

The Clown

As the moon rose in the jet-black sky,
I finished my day with an apple pie.
Just to wake up in a lie, with a face staring,
So I thought he was caring.
So, I went up to him,
Then I realised he was filled to the brim,
With children my age or more,
And he was trying to raise the score.
Eyes were lasers,
Words were tasers.
Nose was red as blood.
Fell, *thud!*
I got up, I ran with dread,
To hopefully not be found dead.
I was in the forest so deep.
Wish I was not in the middle of sleep.
Eyes of lasers came to me,
He was like a killer bee.
So, I ran away, then stopped.
I heard a laugh, then it was all dark
And I woke up next to a lot of bark.

Lola Hill (10)
Springwood Federation (Junior School), Waterlooville

The Wicked Witch

As I settle down to fall to sleep,
I close my eyes and dare not to peep.
What is passing through my mind,
Is a witch that is not very kind.

As black as night,
I know the silhouette wants to fight.
She is a devil, she is a killer,
All she will eat is children for dinner.

Her cloak is a shadow, that is dark,
And her skin is like ancient tree bark.
I turn, I see her standing there,
She's taken me, I'm now in her lair.

With a start, I sit up, wide awake,
My body is trembling, it was a mistake.
I could not,
It was a very bad nightmare.

Niamh Hussey (10)
Springwood Federation (Junior School), Waterlooville

The Disturbing Clown

As I drifted off thinking I'd have a dream,
I fell into a nightmare and let out a scream.
I closed my eyes and dared not to peep,
As I wished not to be asleep.

I thought I was lost,
Oh no, he was coming, my life would come at a cost.
His nose was a shark,
And skin like bark,
He was a murderer, he was a killer,
He only ate children for dinner.

It was too late, my time had come,
I cried, I screamed, my body went numb.
He got me...
As I lay dead like a tree,
There was no escape, I hoped not to be dead,
But then I woke up in my warm bed.

Delilah Dales (10)
Springwood Federation (Junior School), Waterlooville

A Dream You've Had Before

Have you ever seen a witch,
So ugly it made you itch?
Well, a fairy tale is the place,
That has such grace,

A dream you've had before,
When your brain opens a door,
To what seems like another world,
Where magic and wonder is hurled.

Alas, alas, a dream you've had before,
Your brain shall open another door,
Where that door leads is another floor
Where a girl shall steal porridge from a bear,
And a prince shall climb up a girl's hair,

Then your brain shuts the door,
And you're back to where you were before.

Isaac Dixon (9)
Springwood Federation (Junior School), Waterlooville

The Witch Of Horror

As I settled down to go to sleep,
I closed my eyes and dared not peep.
I found myself in a scary park
I saw a little dog that did not bark.
I tried to go, but I felt a hand.
It was gentle now I understand.
Her hat was a snake,
I tried to get awake.
Her dress was like metal,
I saw her warming a kettle.
She said, "You should have not gone to sleep,"
And after, got ready to do a big leap.
I looked at the sky; it was becoming day,
It was about to be my last chance to get away.
She asked if I wanted to play,
But I let go and ran away.
I woke up, hip hip hooray,
I hope it won't happen to me today.

Ano Musa (9)
Springwood Federation (Junior School), Waterlooville

What Is A Witch?

What is a witch?
It flies on a broomstick
Where do they go?
Nobody knows?
They are watery and old
And they fly in the cold
They cast wicked spells
And they push people in wells

Her nose is a shark
And her skin is ancient tree bark
She has blood-red eyes
You will reach your demise
She's incredibly poor
Which means she always breaks
The law
She steals people's cash
And makes herself a stash
She's always in disguise
Which means she always lies
Until I recognised
It was
All a dream.

Charlotte Parker (9)
Springwood Federation (Junior School), Waterlooville

The Witch

As I settled down in my cosy bed,
My mind went out to something else instead.
A witch: warty and old, a cat lead-black,
Lots of bones and skulls in a stack.
What a creature she was, malicious and vicious.
Then came a howling cackle,
And a massive crackle.
A ball of a fire and bunch of sparks,
Followed by some booming barks,
And I woke up in a fright.
The light from my bedroom blinded me from sight.
There stood my mum holding bacon and eggs,
I realised I had very sweaty legs.
But then I realised it was a nightmare, not real life.

Oscar Faux (9)
Springwood Federation (Junior School), Waterlooville

The Demonic Witch

As the moon rose in the dark night,
I closed my eyes from left to right.
As I fell into a nightmare a devious witch,
She stared me down in a ditch.
She was a killer,
All she ate was children for dinner.
Her nose was like a claw crab,
It could snap from drawer to drawer.
Her cloak was a shadow, incredibly dark,
She lived in a lair covered in bark.
I could not run, I could not hide.
This would be a menacing ride,
I woke up in a fright,
I looked left to right.
I burst out in a cry,
Then I found out it was all a lie.

Macie Doughty (10)
Springwood Federation (Junior School), Waterlooville

The Nightmare

As the sun set,
Me and my nightmare met.
I got ready for bed,
In my dreams, I saw a scary head.
The fog appeared surrounding my house,
Gnarled, made me feel like a mouse.
She looked and gave me a vicious smile,
I saw the bones in a pile.
I could not wake up,
I know she would eat me just like a dead pup,
She stared me directly in the face,
Her wand was like a mace.
I couldn't run, I couldn't hide,
I just wanted to be inside.
If she caught me, she would murder me,
But then I woke up, fortunately.

Logan McKenzie (9)
Springwood Federation (Junior School), Waterlooville

The Nightmare

As the moon rose in the night sky,
A dark silhouette caught my eye.
There was a corridor in the dark,
Which had a wardrobe made of bark.
Behind it was a witch as dark as night,
Her skin wasn't bright.
Running after me,
I couldn't hear, I couldn't see.
I shouldn't peep,
Or I must leap.
She was a devil - menacing, evil and a killer,
All she could eat was chicken for dinner.
She grabbed me tightly, I began to scream.
I woke up to my alarm; it was a dream.

Alfie Walker (10)
Springwood Federation (Junior School), Waterlooville

The Witch

The witch was wrinkly and fat
And I'm not about that.
As I looked up the moon rose,
The witch only wore old ragged clothes,
I thought this was a nightmare,
Then I saw a path which led me to her lair,
She was disgusting and warty,
And not at all sporty,
She decided to offer me a pie,
But I thought I'd not die.
Then she threw me in a ditch
And I had a stitch.
Her skin was like tree bark,
She had eyes as red as blood
And I accidentally stood in mud,
She grabbed me and then I woke up in bed,
All snuggly and warm instead.

Dalton Gray (9)
Springwood Federation (Junior School), Waterlooville

Fairy Tale Dream

My head hit the pillow at night,
Full of dreams that caused a fright,
Of courageous and valiant heroes,
And stepmothers with gnarled, curled toes.
It started with a terrible fall,
And a screech of, "You can't go to the ball,
So scrub that wall."
"No!" I screamed. "I want to go to the mall!"
Her gnarled fingers grabbed me on her wrinkled hands,
I didn't think my feet would land.
She had a broom,
That looked like a bomb that would go boom.

Jack Humphreys (9)
Springwood Federation (Junior School), Waterlooville

It's Only A Fairy Tale Dream

Kids are dreaming all around
Of evil witches with hair like straw
And breaking the law
Good take their time making the crime right again
Children drift off into dreams
Where children get trapped by warty witches
With a nose like a crab claw or
Little girls dreaming of princesses trapped in a tower
By an evil malicious witch, making a dish of lies where
Daughters may lie, then children wake up and realise it was only
Once upon a dream.

Isabelle Merrett (10)
Springwood Federation (Junior School), Waterlooville

The Beast

The beast
Frightening dream
Green blood-sucking monster
Creeping into my room, wake up!
Too late
Too late,
The beast got me!
When I saw the beast
It scared my socks off my cheesy feet.
I'm dead,
I'm dead,
I am dinner.
I fade as it stared
I wake up and I sit up, I straighten,
The beast,
The beast opens its mouth
And I quickly run away
It's coming, I run like the wind
I'm gone.

Kyler Speake (9)
Springwood Federation (Junior School), Waterlooville

Once Upon A Time

When my head hits the pillow at night
And the stars above are shining bright,
My mind begins to tell old tales
Of true love and how friendships never fail.
But in tonight's dream,
An evil witch with eyes agleam.
Her hair was rotten straw,
She broke the law
By breaking down a door.
She had a pet lobster
Whose name was Monster,
Her hat was a scorpion tail,
And her skin was really pale.
I woke up in such a fright
And jumped out of bed and turned on the light!

Elsie Lewis (10)
Springwood Federation (Junior School), Waterlooville

The Wicked Witch

While in bed and sleeping tight,
In the middle of the night.
What was passing through my mind,
Was a witch, not very kind.

She asked me if I wanted to play,
But she took me far away.
Was a super scary place,
Somewhere out of space.

Her cat was as night,
Once you see her you will get a fright.
With a start, I sat up wide awake,
My body was trembling, it was a mistake.

Magda Formela (10)
Springwood Federation (Junior School), Waterlooville

Fire Sorcerer

Light a fire to the sorcerer's delight,
The eeriest dream of all the scary nights.
Fire flares, a silhouette destroyer, screaming,
I really hope that I am dreaming.
A hand grabs me and gives me a vicious bite,
Struggling for freedom, I run into the night.
I find a secret overgrown hideout,
I hope he won't find out.
I realise now I'm in a dream,
Probably because of that scary meme.

Darius Kidykas (9)
Springwood Federation (Junior School), Waterlooville

The Wicked Witch

While in bed, asleep and tight,
In the middle of the night.
What was passing through my magical mind,
Was a wicked witch, not very kind.
She asked if I wanted to play,
But her hair was all old and grey.
It was a super scary place somewhere,
Out of space,
When she put her bony fingers on my shoulder,
I felt her move closer and closer,
I woke up with a scream and it was a bad dream.

Isaac Bennett (9)
Springwood Federation (Junior School), Waterlooville

The Witch

The witch was hunting.
Stalking my dreams.
She was a murderer, the devil.
I must run quickly.
She was coming as black as the night sky,
A frightening, horrible sight.
She was here, she found me.
There was no escape.
Her pointed teeth like daggers.
Please don't hurt me.
Her mouth as big as she can.
I managed to get out, I ran.
I hoped this was just a nightmare.

Katherine Scott (10)
Springwood Federation (Junior School), Waterlooville

Untitled

Today I was mean
So I fell into a dream
About a giant
And he had a well
And in that well he had some money
And he had a pet which was a witch
And it really liked honey
Its name was Bear
And it had lots of hair
Like a polar bear
Jack came in
His axe went swing
As the beanstalk went *bing*
As the bell went *ting*
As I woke up with a fright.

Max Northall (9)
Springwood Federation (Junior School), Waterlooville

The Witch

As I settled down to fall asleep,
I closed my eyes and dared not to peep.
Heading off into the depths of my mind,
I knew she was coming; I just needed to find.
She was a devil, she was a killer,
All she would eat is children for dinner.
The spike on her hat
Was like a little rat.
Her black hair,
Gave me quite a scare.
As she grabbed my arm,
I woke up to my alarm.

Annie-May Lines (9)
Springwood Federation (Junior School), Waterlooville

Untitled

Once upon a time, a witch did a crime.
Her skin was like an arid tree bark.
Her cloak was midnight dark.
She flicks her wand and goes into your dreams.
Don't trust her ways.
She doesn't work as a team.
She was evil and mean.
She was always faking to be a teen.
But things aren't always what they seem.

Amelia Coombes (9)
Springwood Federation (Junior School), Waterlooville

Drifting Into Dreams

Fairies flying
Evil dying
Kingdoms dreaming
People gleaming
Evil does a crime
At the right time
Light guides you back home
But witches roam
Witches have warts
But that's what you're taught
Dreams become nightmares in a click
Witches fly on their broomsticks really quick.

Elise Goolty (10)
Springwood Federation (Junior School), Waterlooville

A Tale For The Night

I fall on my pillow in the night,
Trying to sleep without a fright.
But far, far away in my mind,
A tragic story, I find.
Emerging from the void,
A girl was seen sweeping, looking annoyed.
She had a stepmother with a scorpion on her head,
Her wicked soul would never care if her daughter was dead.

Ana Makepeace (10)
Springwood Federation (Junior School), Waterlooville

Fairy Tale Dreams

Today I saw a meme,
So it made me dream,
About a witch
Who was rich.

Her name is Jill,
She never paid her bill.
Her hair is a storm,
It goes against the norm.

Her nails as long as a branch,
Her hair smells like ranch.
She lives in Chile,
She is a bit silly.

Scarlett Prince (10)
Springwood Federation (Junior School), Waterlooville

The Witch

Under moonlight,
From her candy cane house,
In the big forgotten forest,
The dark.

The dark
Wrinkly skin,
A cold-blooded demon,
Her dark magical hat,
Scary.

Scary,
She held in her red
With yellow nails her grasp was strong,
I scream.

George Needham (9)
Springwood Federation (Junior School), Waterlooville

A Fairy Tale Dream

Beneath my bed
All feathered and red
Lies a cackling witch
Who makes me itch
I lift my head
Thinking I'm dead
Then lifts her wand and... *Bang!*
Cave bats start to hang
My mind begins to wonder
When I'll leave this deep slumber.

Frederick Carter-Brazier (10)
Springwood Federation (Junior School), Waterlooville

The Witch

Oh no, I beg,
A witch with a black cat,
A broom, a hat,
I cannot run, I cannot hide,
Full of shock, it's a ride.
I know I am dead, as this time I dread,
I scream, I come,
I cry, my body goes numb.
It was just a nightmare.

Louis Cole (10)
Springwood Federation (Junior School), Waterlooville

Once I Had A Dream

Once, I had a dream
Of cruel villains in a team
The malicious main leader
Was not kind, dear reader
With rotten straw as hair
It could be in a nightmare

Her eyes were red
Never to dread
Her nose was a claw
As sharp as a crab claw.

Phoebe Spencer (9)
Springwood Federation (Junior School), Waterlooville

Untitled

While I was dreaming,
The stars were gleaming
Of a witch from Chile
Who felt silly
She was cool
But had never been in a pool
Her arms were trees
But were small like bees
Her name was Gill
She never paid the bill.

Harry Clements (10)
Springwood Federation (Junior School), Waterlooville

Once Upon A Dream

Once upon a time
A witch did a crime
Her skin was ancient tree bark
And her cloak was midnight dark
Which danced along the ground
And she snuck around without a single sound.

Madeleine Parker (9)
Springwood Federation (Junior School), Waterlooville

The Doll

Its creepy face,
Little kids come to her
Her clothes are as black as a cat
She floats
You can not run
She is an evil killer
She is a devil
I know I am her dinner.

Mia Worcester (10)
Springwood Federation (Junior School), Waterlooville

Little Girl

D eep in the forest
R ed Riding Hood lived
E arly in the morning
A wolf appeared
M y grandma disappeared.

George Johnson (9)
Springwood Federation (Junior School), Waterlooville

Football Dreams

I was at a match in my dream.
I was watching my favourite team go by with a swoosh and a boot.
My life flashed before my eyes, I heard a boot and a slam.
Next thing I knew, I was cheering as loud as a lion.
I threw myself around in excitement
I was over the moon.
All the fans were cheering with laughter and enjoyment.
The stadium was so full,
I felt like it was about to explode.
So hot.
So cramped.
Still cheering on and on,
The ball was being kicked about, and then *bam!*
It went in the goal again.
The stadium was roaring like a pack of lions.
They were all laughing at the opposite team.
When the match was over, I saw a bunch of people laughing and having lots of fun.
I smelled burgers.
I was hungry.

Florence Parker (10)
The Russell School, Rickmansworth

Go Wild With Lego

Lego building is fun for me,
On my own or with my family,
Strange new worlds or Mario,
Can all be built with blocks of Lego,

Educational and lots of fun,
Even if you get it wrong,
Trying hard is all you have to do,
Let your imagination go wild, won't you?

Big, red blocks put a smile on my face
In my bedroom or at a friend's place,
The perfect creation is my quest,
Lego building is the *best!*

Theodore Peter Smith (10)
The Russell School, Rickmansworth

Wonders

I find myself in fields so vast,
Surrounded by animals galloping fast.
Happiness lights the rainbow sky,
One by one they pass me by.
Joy is bouncing in my heart,
The animals suddenly move apart,
And as I look around I see,
Surely something that cannot be.
The cabins stand with pride so strong,
I suddenly notice the sweet birdsong.
Lanterns beam with light so bright,
As soon as they see it, the birds take flight.

Ben Collett (10)
The Russell School, Rickmansworth

Once Upon A Dream

Every night, a different dream
I wonder which one it may be
Eating a snail or baking a cake
Each night is different, just you wait
A talking dog with fancy wings
An action figure might start to sing
Anything is possible
Just put your head on the pillow
And you may find you're talking to a weeping willow!

Emily Raine (10)
The Russell School, Rickmansworth

Stargazer

Once upon a dream,
I believed I could be seen,
Disguised as a million different things
I want to feel the joy it brings.

I want to be an actress
I want to be a star
I want to prove I can go far.

I will use the Scarecrow's brain
And the Tin Man's heart
To build courage like the Lion
And give my dream the best start.

Once upon a dream
I believe I could be seen
My first show was about to begin
I practised my lines and found the star within.

My words are not mine
My clothes of a different time
I am not nervous, I can't wait to start
This is my chance to play the perfect part.

At the end of the show, I can hear the cheer
A spotlight beaming on me
I feel like I am the only one here.

The sound keeps ringing in my ear
And the lights get more and more clear.

The star from night-time is far away
It is the start of a brand new day.

Lyla Keeling (10)
Widewell Primary School, Widewell

Was It Just A Nightmare?

N obody was there but it felt like someone was watching.
I suddenly heard a creak of a door and footsteps were getting closer.
G lancing left and right, my heart started to drop.
"H ello!" I said, but there was no answer.
"T urn around," whispered a deep voice. I quickly shot around but no one was there.
M y heart began to drop and my breathing got heavier.
A scary, wrinkly hand grabbed my wrist, making me scream!
R unning as fast as lightning, I tried to find my way out.
E ventually, I found a door that led to a fog-covered forest.
S uddenly, I woke up, cosy in my bed and it was finally over, or so I thought.

Jessica Cook (11)
Widewell Primary School, Widewell

Peace For All

I dream of a world where peace is all around,
All races friends,
Where happiness is found.
I dream of a world where all religions work together,
Different colours shaking hands,
No more war, even in the darkest weather.
I dream of a world where all genders are equal,
The planet is safe,
That's my perfect sequel.
I dream of a world where all children are happy,
All bullies defeated,
Just the thought makes me so hopeful I'm flappy!
Then I yawn and I stretch and I sit up in bed,
And I think of my dream, equally led.
I think to myself about what the world's like right now,
No, it's not perfect,
But we can make it sound!

Poppy Rebhan (11)
Widewell Primary School, Widewell

Nightmare

I had a dream
It was very mean
I think it was a nightmare
Not that you would care
Surrounded by smoke
This must be a joke
But what's that in the distance?
There is a presence
Fire blazing all around me
I can't see
A blur going red and orange
Moving around will be a challenge
That man is getting closer
Oh no, he's coming over
I blink and open my eyes
Luckily, it was all lies.

Chloe Ball (10)
Widewell Primary School, Widewell

Dream Horses

D ream, dream, go to sleep. Dream about all those lovely dream horses.
R iding high up the massive hill deep into my dreams, flying high up in the sky because of my dream.
E questrian riders ride through town, talking and giggling as they ride downtown.
A dmiring the magical horse as it flies down the path; sparkles, shimmers, dashes, and goes to the stable. Fly, fly, fly!
M agical footprints in the sky, trotting through the fluffy clouds.

H orses galloping through the woods.
O h no, someone fell off. Don't worry, I'm okay!
R unning through the silky grass, ending the day.
S eeing each bit of the sun go down, magic fills the dot.
E asing.

Thea Gentry (9)
Woburn Lower School, Woburn

My Peculiar Dream

I dreamt I was in the clouds.
But every day I had a frown
Because I knew I was busy.
I didn't know
What to show
Or where to go.
But people brought in fizzes.
Although I said, "No!"
Dreading my only fear.
It is very close.
I saw the King and Queen with beer!
I saw some strange people having a boast.
Oh no, those strange people and some *ghosts!*
But I quickly opened my eyes.
With fairies, unicorns, my mum and dad.
The King and Queen of Florida.
And I was in my four-poster bed.
Knowing in my bed what my next book would be!
And in the end, I was a famous writer.
In the royal family with everything I ever wanted.

Harper Quinn Grady (7)
Woburn Lower School, Woburn

Fought Or Fight?

F ought on the battlefield with all my might
O r I can go and die tonight,
U nder the wall, I hide with all my soldiers,
G ot most of them to hide so tight
H ot stuff flew through the air
T onight was a bright night.

O ut of the sky people glide
R ound where I hide people glide,

F ields and fields blood lay
I and people who survived
G ot hurt, but survived,
H igh and low people hide
T oday people lie in the grave.

Malaki Godsall (9)
Woburn Lower School, Woburn

One Night In My Dreams

One night in my dream,
It was very extreme.

There were lakes, trees,
And great big seas.

With no loud cars but beautiful stars.
And magnificent beasts who loved big feasts.

Then I realised I was in the sky,
Because I could fly.

I flew higher and higher into the sky
And I thought, *is this a lie?*

Suddenly, I fell to the ground and heard my name
Then I woke up and went, "Oh, it was just a dream."

Hamish (9)
Woburn Lower School, Woburn

The Magic Box

I was going to my grandma's house
To stay there for a week.
I packed my stuff to go.
We got into the car, it was a long journey.
I fell asleep!

I had a dream about a magic box
Of fairies in a winter wonderland.

I will put them in the box.
A crystal cream, crinkly crop top.
A flock of flying, flickering fairies
And a fairy's wand.

They got there and I said to her,
"Mum, I had the nicest dream."

Freya Williams (9)
Woburn Lower School, Woburn

My Dream

Once I was in bed,
I held on so tight!
I scratched my head,
And then said, "Oh, that sight!"
I just saw a flash of light!

Suddenly, I jumped out of bed.
My eyes gleamed at one sight!
It was a flying reindeer
On Christmas night.

I shouted, "Woo, ahh!"
But then I thought to myself,
Why could I hear Santa and his elf?!
I said, "I need to be asleep!"
And then, oh no, I woke up!

Olivia Smith (8)
Woburn Lower School, Woburn

Untitled

Inspired by The Magic Box by Kit Wright

I dreamt I put into my magic box
The stinkiest nail of an ogre from Japan.
A rotten bat wing from Australia,
The snot of a dragon.

I dreamt I put into my magic box
The kind man was whistling,
The leaf man was drumming,
The man had a stomach ache.

I dreamt I put into my magic box
The deathly roar from the Atlantic dragon
The feather of a phoenix.

I dreamt I put into my magic box
A fool's gold
And ice on the lid
Snake fangs on the corner.

Jake Farmer (7)
Woburn Lower School, Woburn

Killer Clowns

When I went up to the attic
I found a box that sucked me in
And I heard a funny sound...
Killer clowns!

I went down and down
Until I finished.
I got dished on a plate
And I had a mate.
His name was Cobi
And he was quite dopey.

I ran and ran until I found a van,
And I got away until the next day.
It was only a nightmare
So don't swear!

Logan Christie (8)
Woburn Lower School, Woburn

Day In The Life With A Bunny

B ye! Got to go home! I'm getting a bunny today!
U h oh! It pooped, and now I have to clean it up.
N ow I have to feed it; that should be fun, except if she goes to Mum.
N ow it's time to go to bed.
Y es! It's morning, time to get fed. So that's the life with a bunny. Cool, I guess. Bye! Getting a dog so watch the next one!

Genevieve Butler (9)
Woburn Lower School, Woburn

Pet Store

Once I was in the pet store
with my Labrador
called Thor.

He needed a friend to have some fun,
but they didn't notice it was right in the sun.
They saw kittens, puppies,
and more!
But nothing,
just nothing,
suited good Thor.
The animal in the sun long ago wished to be sold,
but nobody wanted him because he was
dirty!

Katalea Butler (7)
Woburn Lower School, Woburn

Untitled

F luttering my wings
A nd jumping on my things.
I love dancing with fairies!
R uby, Lexie, Pixie and Chloe.
Y ou can come too, but it's a little bit snowy. So we danced all night long.

D rumming to a song
A nd having fun.
N o one was there. How
C an I get
E nchanted?

Violet Whitmore (8)
Woburn Lower School, Woburn

Footballer

F ootballs fit in my garden.
O h no, too many footballs.
O h no, that's better!
T oo much better, maybe.
B ags of West Ham flags,
A big bag of Tottenham flags.
L oving the start of the game.
L oving the end of the game!
E ating hot dogs at home.
R iding a bike the next day.

Harley Walton-Payne (7)
Woburn Lower School, Woburn

Badland

I woke up.

B ells rang, drums drummed and I woke.
A hhh! I saw the eroded Badlands.
D oh! I'm in the eroded Badlands.
L ots of black.
A swamp! Yay! Water! I jumped in.
N o! A kraken! I killed it!
D o I see a gem? I took it.

I woke up.

Felix Howard (7)
Woburn Lower School, Woburn

Famous

F lashing camera lights, everywhere.
A utographs; I've done so many!
M ovies, shows, I've done them all.
O bviously, I know it's just a dream.
U nderneath my covers, it feels like a stage.
S o fun! Oh no! I woke up!

Elodie Clarke (9)
Woburn Lower School, Woburn

My Summer Holidays

A ll day, I would go to the beach.
L ong days pass by,
B ands are playing everywhere.
A ll day, licking my ice cream!
N othing spoils the day!
I will always love playing in the sun.
A ll day, I will run and play!

Amy Bezh (7)
Woburn Lower School, Woburn

YoungWriters®
Est. 1991

YOUNG WRITERS INFORMATION

We hope you have enjoyed reading this book – and that you will continue to in the coming years.

If you're a young writer who enjoys reading and creative writing, or the parent of an enthusiastic poet or story writer, do visit our website **www.youngwriters.co.uk**. Here you will find free competitions, workshops and games, as well as recommended reads, a poetry glossary and our blog.

If you would like to order further copies of this book, or any of our other titles, then please give us a call or visit **www.youngwriters.co.uk**.

Young Writers
Remus House
Coltsfoot Drive
Peterborough
PE2 9BF
(01733) 890066
info@youngwriters.co.uk

 YoungWritersUK   **YoungWritersCW**
 youngwriterscw   **youngwriterscw**